James Wilkerson

Wilkerson's History of His Travels and Labors, in the United States

James Wilkerson

Wilkerson's History of His Travels and Labors, in the United States

ISBN/EAN: 9783337207335

Printed in Europe, USA, Canada, Australia, Japan

Cover: Foto ©Andreas Hilbeck / pixelio.de

More available books at **www.hansebooks.com**

WILKERSON'S

HISTORY

OF HIS

TRAVELS & LABORS,

In the United States,

AS A MISSIONARY,

IN PARTICULAR, THAT OF

The Union Seminary,

LOCATED IN FRANKLIN CO. OHIO,

Since he purchased his Liberty in New Orleans, La., &c.

———————

COLUMBUS, OHIO.
1861.

PREFACE, OR INTRODUCTION.

Columbus, Ohio, 11th of 11th Month, A. D. 1860.

To THE CHRISTIAN COMMUNITY, AND THE PUBLIC IN GENERAL.

The writer has here thought fit, in compliance with the request of his worthy friend Wright, the Conductor of the Wilberforce Institute, Ohio, to write out a brief Narrative, as the nature of the case will permit, as it may be both interesting and satisfactory to many of his loving readers. Even so, amen, and selah.

Oh, ye lovely and tender brood,
May your mother ever find you food,
And may you ever to her arms prove true,
In all you act, or say or do.
And while you live upright in heart,
To you her bounty she is bound to impart.
Thus under her wings you may safely rest,
In leaning on her lovely breast;
For surely to all her sons that's free,
She secures to them their liberty,
And faithfully administers her laws to all,
That does on her for justice call.
Therefore little flock you need not fear,
While her Love and Justice is near,
For her wings are large and truly strong,
To defend and shield you from every wrong.
Then to her banner may you in heart ascribe,
With it to live and ever abide ;
And not for silver or British gold,
Like B. Arnold let your trust be sold.

And now, in the outset, the writer would notice in the first place his having purchased his liberty in New Orleans, La. as strictly set forth in the Midnight Cry, say on or about the 10th of 6th month, A. D. 1835, and after that of his mother, in Petersburg, Va.; and he being then a member of the M. E. Church, he continued in said church as a local minister thereof, for some two or three years. But by this he thought fit to meet with the Conference of the African M. E. Church, in Cincinnati, Ohio, say on or about the 25th of 8th month, A. D. 1838; hence, it was then and there he did join said Conference, under the administration of the worthy head and Superintendent of said Church, namely, M. B. of Philadelphia, Pa. Hence, he now having become a member thereof, he was duly appointed by said Conference as a Missionary, acting in a coequal sphere with their then Missionary in the West, namely, W. P. Q., we being aided by our Brother, G. W. J. Hence, be it known by all of his loving readers, that it was from thence did the writer's unremitting labours of love commence, in behalf of God's poor, in the establishing of Churches and Schools, under the patronage of said Conference, say throughout the West, yea, and even in the South, say as far down as New Orleans, the writer's old and esteemed home. Even so, let God be praised in this, for his aid on the part of his servants in their efforts to establish his holy cause, as in the case of his servants of old, namely, Daniel, Shadrach, Meshach, and Abednego, when exiles down in Babylon. But oh! in this effort on the part of the writer, as to his labours and great sacrifices, is it not strictly written out in his major Journal, of about forty years history or more.

Hence, this great and glorious enterprise being thus accomplished, and that to the honor and glory of God, and of no little joy, yea, inexpressibly so on the part of his Colored Brethren and friends of said city; and for which Christian privileges, may they to appreciate them, that God may be pleased to grant their continuance; yea, and to be watchful unto prayer, and to see that no wolves from abroad, in sheep's clothing, enter into their midst to annoy their peace again. Even, so, for why should your peace be thus molested, oh, ye house of Israel, and little flock of the Most High God? Even as in the case of God's people of old, when in exile from Jerusalem down to Babylon, &c., &c.

Next, the writer was solicited by the Trustees of the African M. E. Church, of Indianapolis, Ind., to act as an Agent for them to solicit aid of the public to save, if possible, their church and school-house from being sold for debt. And here, when upon reflection of their pitiful condition, he could not, it seemed, for his soul, pass them by without letting them have his aid in this case. Hence, he having concluded to act for them as before named, he commenced on this his mission, say on or about the 20th of 9th month, 1842; hence it was after some fifteen months or more of his hard labours in the cold and heat, he truly succeeded in securing of said property, safely into the hands of said Trustees, in the behalf of said church. Even so, let God be truly praised for having aided his servant thus, for otherwise, it seems to the writer, that it would have been about his last effort in this world, or trying to aid his fellow creatures in going about doing good, from the fact that he got frost bitten some several times, and besides, he had inward fever and a severe cough for several weeks; yea, so much so, that he was made to think that he was about done with time and sense as to this world. But here it seemed to please God that his servant's bodily affliction should not be in this case unto death, nay, nay. Hence, he having recovered his health again, he concluded to go over to the East, and there to join some one of the Conferences, say probably that of Baltimore, Md., as said city has ever been one of his most favored rights in all of the Union, so far as it concerns his ministerial privileges, even so; but we pass by saying by this his daughter Julia was born on 23d of 8th month, 1843, say, and may she become as in the case of Rebecca of old before the God of all the righteous, amen.

And now, having honorably acquitted himself of said Trustees, before a Justice of the Peace, in this matter, he took his leave of his loving friends of said city. But whilst on his way to the East with his wife and child, namely, his dear little Julia, he met with three certain brethren, namely, W. P. Q., M. M. C. and W. R. R., at Cambridge, Ind., and there and then was the writer most earnestly solicited by said brethren, not to leave the West yet, by any means whatever, stating as there was yet another and most worthy of all benevolent objects under contemplation, by the Ohio Conference, namely, the establishing of a School upon a Manual Labour plan, that should serve in three points of view. namely.

a Home for the poor wornout Ministers of said Conference, as well as an Orphan Institute, yea, and besides these, where young men who might feel themselves called to the Ministry, should have an opportunity of working out their board and education. Even so, amen. And further stating that said Conference had already made choice of the writer as a proper person to act for them as an Agent and Attorney in fact, provided that he would serve as such. And here it was, notwithstanding the writer had truly thought within his soul that the mission before named should have been his last here upon earth; but when upon due reflection of the said three points, in view of which said Institute should serve, yea, and that of the very plan adopted by the worthy and ever memorable John Wesley, the Father and Founder of Methodism in its outset, in the behalf of the Ministry, that there should be no reproach attached thereunto in regard to the wants of the Ministers' families, in case of their being absent on their circuits or missions, say, for several months or more, as the nature of the case might be on their part. as faithful and devoted heralds of the consecrated Cross of Christ, in wrestling or resisting the powers of the Prince of this World, or to be plain, the Arch Fiend of Hell, whose daily object is to annul and bring to nought the kingdom of the Prince of Peace and Everlasting Glory. Hence, to be successful in this, all of said Ministers that would come and vow to serve thus, should take their families to said Institute that was thus provided; yea, and there leave them all to share together, having all things in common, as in the days of the Apostles, excepting those who might have means of their own to do otherwise, even so. Hence, it was after this very wise, it truly seems, did the good old time Methodism proceed in carrying out the vital piety and the true orthodox principles of religion; yea, and like unto the mighty stone that Daniel saw cut out of the mountain, without hands, rolling and crushing as it were everything that might oppose it, even so. But oh! where is said Methodism now, in teaching of said loving and God-fearing principles, in this the year of our Lord, 1861?

Hence, he having here come to the conclusion to serve said Conference in said mission, yea, though it might prove to him a lifetime effort; even so, seeing that in so doing that, it was but a strict religious act of duty on his part, provided, that he would meet the sayings of St. James the Apostle, thus, thou shalt visit the widows in their affliction, and to take care of the Fatherless, and walking unspotted of the world, and in this, says said Apostle, is true and genuine religion. Even so, amen, and selah, responds the writer, in attest of the fact thereof. Amen.

And now, he having pledged to said brethren, that he would serve as before named, and taking his leave of them, he came next to Richmond, Ind., where he found the Yearly Meeting of Friends, commonly called Quakers, in session, and which he, of course, could not well pass, until the adjournment of said meeting; and in so doing, he had the inexpressible pleasure of calling on many of said Friends, yea, and in particular, that of his old time friend, and family, E. C., yea, one from whose door he never departed empty handed—nay, nay; hence, of all the writer's loving friends, said family is not surpassed, nay, even by one of his most warm and worthy friends that now survives in New Orleans, La., namely, the Ex-Attorney General, T. C., of Louisiana. Hence, to the former and the latter named friends, the writer is here truly at a loss for the want of words to express his lasting gratitude to them; hence, let it suffice for him to say, may the Lord his God ever bless them accordingly. Yea, and not forgetting all others in the way of reckoning up his precious jewels, on his arrival in our world the second time; as it is written, that not a cup of cold water that may have been administered unto one of his disciples, should go unrewarded. Even so, God grant it.

And now, said Yearly Meeting of Friends having adjourned, *sine die*, the writer concluded to renew his sojourn for his destiny, even to this the capital of the before-named State, and he having arrived here, say on or about the 20th of 10th month, A. D. 1844, and he having called the Committee together, that had been appointed by said Conference to act with him in this matter, namely, Thomas Lawrence, M. T. Newsom, and Lewis Adams, he found, to his great surprise, that there had not been the first cent appropriated by said Conference, or even a book, with its preface setting forth the object of their wishes, or claims upon a Christian community, by which they, the Conference, might be rightly represented, &c., only stating that the writer, their brother, had been duly elected as their Agent and Attorney in fact, provided that he would serve as such, simply stating a mere theory of their object, as before named, &c. &c. Hence, to all of his loving readers, judge

ye for yourselves in this case, and say, that if your humble penman was not left as it were, to create a mountain solely with his
ten finger nails, or resort to his own pocket, and so equip himself
out for his mission that was conferred upon him by said Conference; or to pass the whole matter by, and so go on his way, as
in the case of the Priest and the holy Levites, so called, when on
their way up to Jerusalem, being as does seem, in so great a haste
for the golden fleece, that they had not time to remember the poor
man whom they saw on the way, that was not only robbed of all
he had, but was beaten, as it seemed, until his very bones stared
him in the face. Say, and where are the Priests and Levites in
this our day and age of the world? say 5864 years since the day
in which the morning stars sang together, and the sons of God
shouted for joy—in the formation of this, another new world; even
so, amen, and selah. Say, are there no such characters as in the
pitiful case of said man? and besides, thousands of poor widows
and orphans in this our so called Christian land, looking up and im-
portuning with tears in their eyes, yea, and crying for bread daily
in the streets of our cities, yea, even from Jackson's Monument,
New Orleans, La. to Bunker Hill, Boston, Mass., that would truly
like to have their attention, if said Priests and Levites be not too
much engaged in securing of farms, houses and lots, for themselves,
and that solely by the fleecing of God's poor; say, loving readers,
and will not God, in his righteous judgments, speedily cleanse his
Holy Temple from all such infamous infamy? answer, he will, if
he has not commenced already in routing the lying spirit of that of
an Ananias and his wife Sapphira. Even so, amen; and let all of
his humble saints praise Him for this his helping hand, in lifting up
their dejected heads, looking from whence their redemption shall
speedily come: even so, may God in his goodness let it come. .
Amen. Hallelujah!

And now, said Committee and the writer, having made choice
of a suitable tract of land of about 180 acres, located on the
waters of Darby, Franklin County, Ohio, it having some little
improvement thereon, and they now having contracted with the
owners thereof, namely, S. D. and G., say for ten dollars per
acre, with interest from date of the contract, hence the next thing
was for said Committee to be acknowledged before his honour,
'Squire M., as the proper Trustees, acting in the behalf of said

Conference, and they, on their part, acknowledging the writer to be their Agent and Attorney in fact. Hence, this being duly attended to, the writer now calls on the Clerk of the Court of Common Pleas, namely, the worthy S., and here he having obtained the Power of an Attorney, in order to act as before named, and for all of said proceedings did he pay for out of his own pocket, trusting solely to a future day for his pay, he having claimed of said Trustees one-third of all that he might collect of the public, and of said one-third, to defray all of his expenses, the same being ratified by the ensuing Conference agreeing that the writer should have said amount for his services, so long as he acted as before named—even so.

And now, the writer being duly equipped for his mission, he commenced by opening his Book of Subscription in this city, and afterwards, he made a general tour throughout the entire district of said Conference. Hence, he having thus opened his Subscription Book to the Colored community first, and this being done, and having his subscribers all to understand, that for said subscription he would call on them annually, until they had met their obligation, &c. Hence, this being so far successfully attended to, he saw nothing lacking further on his part, but time, patience and perseverance to accomplish this object of no little merit, if duly appreciated by whom the writer had thus obligated himself to serve; even so. Next the writer thought it best to hasten on to the East, even to West Philadelphia, Pa., with his family, where he happily situated them under the care of friends, namely, sister N. M. But now C., B. H. & D. G. And here it was that his son Joseph was born, say on or about the 20th of 12th month, Anno Domini, 1845—And may the God of his father, yea, and that of good old Abraham, Isaac and Jacob, and of all the true and faithful to his holy cause, bless the youth, as in the case of his servant Joseph, when an exile down in the land of Egypt, and of that of his father the writer, when an exile from his native land, even old Virginia, down to New Orleans, La.—Even so mote it be—Amen. God save the child, that he may be a comfort to his mother, a blessing to his sister, and great honour to his dear old father, esteeming a precious name more than all this low world can afford.

Now the writer having faithfully discharged his duty in behalf of his domestic affairs, as before named, he returned for the West, and here, in his most punctual attention to duty, in having made some two or three rounds, he came out among his colored friends and subscribers, just as he thought, in subscriptions enough collected to meet, say the first, second, third, and fourth notes—even so—which of course went to encourage the writer much ; yea, so much so, that he thought that he would now give his white friends a call, on behalf of his Agency, having something on his Book to show them of the liberal patronage of his colored friends, &c. But here, to be successful in this, as there were so many imposters out upon the good patience of the public, some to purchase wife and children, and by the time they got the amount required, run off with some other woman or man's wife, whilst others about ditto, he concluded in the first place, to call on the worthy clergy of this city, and have them endorse his credentials first, so that he might have proper access to the pulpits when abroad—even so. And this being done, he next thought fit to call on his Honour, Gov. Z. F., and the worthy Ex Gov. W. B. being present, and he having there and then rightly laid his mission before them, yea, and having stated to them the many disadvantages under which the colored population of this State had to labour, in particular, that in not having access to the Public School Fund, and their testimony in Court, whilst the writer, when at home in New Orleans, was entitled to his in any Court thereof, yea, and besides, all the free population throughout the State of Louisiana, and for which, may the blessings of Almighty God ever rest upon such a Court of Justice to the human family ; yea, and success, in that of peace and lasting prosperity to the officials thereof.

But here, as to the great sympathy manifested in this, on the part of those worthy gentlemen, and of the said Governor's intention of what he would recommend in his inaugural address to the Legislature. As touching said disadvantages, he need not here name, only to let it suffice for him to say, and have they, the said population, now got access to the said School Fund, and their testimony in Court, or not? answer, they have, and may said inexpressible privileges be duly appreciated on their part, and not forgetting to invoke God's blessing upon said Chiefs in office, and the Assembly who have acted thus, in the behalf of God's poor. Even so, amen, and selah.

And now, having had his credentials also endorsed by said Governor and Ex Governor, will of course, attest the fact of said interview, and of the moving cause of said privileges being granted, &c. Hence, he being thus recommended, he now concluded to make a trip East in behalf of his mission, say, commencing at Washington, D. C. ; and whilst there, he called on the Hon. C. D. and J. R. G., then Representatives in Congress from this State, and they having frankly indorsed said documents, yea, acknowledging all of the before-named signatures to be genuine. Next he called upon one of his most distinguished friends of all he claims in this world, namely, B , the District Attorney, yea, the same who acted as counsel for the humble penman, in the emancipation of his mother, he having purchased her, as before named, free of all cost. And for said benevolent act, the writer is here at a loss for the want of words to express his lasting gratitude to said attorney ; therefore, let it suffice for him to say, may God reward him accordingly. And having received counsel of said attorney, whilst there, how he should proceed in his mission, &c., he concluded that he would commence by giving a call upon the colored churches in general, say, by beginning at the great Metropolis of the United States, and so on from city to city, until he reached Boston, Mass. But in this contemplated route, he is here truly sorry to have it to record, that he met with no little opposition throughout all Bethel, or said A. M. E. Church, excepting Washinton and Baltimore. The excuse was on the part of the Ministers thereof, that they wanted just such an institute for their poor ministers and orphans. But here, if the writer may be permitted to speak out his mind, it was rather their poor dirty pockets, that seems in truth to have no bottom, from the very fact that their wants were all duly supplied, in talking of it, sufficient to prevent the proper access that the writer might have had ; yea, so much so, that if it had not been for his friendly Baptist Brother Ministers, and those of other denominations, he would have come far short of his realization in collecting funds in said proposed route. But here let God be praised for his present aid in the time of need, from the fact that said opposition only went to create no little sympathy, yea, and many friends on the part of the writer ; yea, so much so, that on his return here he was enabled to lift the fifth and last note due upon said property, yea, and besides, to pay up all the back tax that was due thereon, &c.—Even so, amen and amen—to wit, Hanson Johnson, Treasurer thereof. And here the concern became incorporated, and other Trustees appointed for the Institute, &c.

And now, what next? answer, Books for the use of said U. Seminary, and materials for the erection of some several good log buildings, in addition to those that were already on the farm; and besides, some several hundred dollars more was required in the completion thereof, before the true and devoted penman could consider himself honorably acquitted from his most arduous field of unremitting labours, as already named. Hence, by this his loving readers may all plainly see, that their humble and obedient servant was left in this case to tread as it were, the winepress alone; for of the brethren of said Conference, none was found to aid of all the Itinerants thereof, but M. M. C., five dollars in cash, D. S. fifty cents, and A. R. G. two dollars, in the way of feeding of his horse, when in Pittsburg, Pa., on his agency, which stands on the book of Subscription until this day, if it is not expunged therefrom. Hence, we pass.

And now, in regard to the collections in said books, and materials for said contemplated Institute, he of course, in this called on his white friends and neighbours, who did contribute liberally, yea, some as high, in books, when collecting in Cincinnati, Ohio, as $60 and $75, namely, from two book sellers, M. and S., Main Street, and not forgetting his honour, T. C., of Lebanon, O., who donated from his own Library about $40 worth, in behalf of God's poor—even so. Hence, be it known to all who may happen to read this, the writer's Narrative, that it was after this wise did the writer collect, say about four or five thousand volumes of books, besides about four hundred dollars in materials—even so. But here, in return in the way of thankfulness to his white brethren and friends for this act of kindness to him in his efforts to do good, whilst this side of yonder sleeping grave that awaits him, yea, and the appointed house for all the living, he is at a loss for the want of words to express; therefore, they will please to let it suffice for him to say, and may the God of all goodness bless them all, yea, individually and collectively—even so mote it be.

But alas, alas! comes the winding up stroke of the writer's unremitting labours and hard struggling for six long years, in the completion of the most desired object for which he engaged his services as before named, and for no other on earth would he have laboured thus—nay, nay—only he having seen that the greater the object that was to be obtained, even so in proportion must needs be the sacrifice; even so—say, as in the case of the worthy and immortalized George Washington, when in battling six years for the inexpressible liberties of this highly favored land and nation, yea, even from Jackson's Monument, New Orleans, La. to Bunker Hill, Boston, Mass., if duly appreciated by those on whom it was conferred; yea, that will tell for itself in ages to come— even so mote it be. Hence, it was in this six years unremitting struggling did it truly seem to please God, the author of all love and liberty, to look down in compassion upon said noted Chieftain, and having taken the will for the deed, he crowned him with the victory in a complete triumph, and so gave to him rest on the seventh year from his many and bitter conflicts that awaited him on every side, as his history will truly show; hence, may his precious soul this day be at rest with God in heaven, and that it may be written over his head thus:—"Write, Blessed are the dead which die in the Lord from henceforth: Yea, saith the Spirit, that they may rest from their labours, and their works do follow them." Yea, in great blessings upon the human family, when duly appreciated, &c.

Hence, there being yet another round of duty that awaited the almost broken down agent, the collection of some several hundred dollars for the erection of several good log buildings on said farm, in addition to those already thereon; so that all of said ministers of said Conference might move thereon with their families, and so meet the great and inexpressible object for which it was truly intended by the writer, and other fathers of said Conference, who now lie sleeping in their peaceful graves, who would have no doubt rejoiced to have seen the day of its completion, but died without the sight. But in this his last winding up or finishing stroke, hear, oh heaven, and bear record, oh earth! of the deathly struggles of one poor mortal who yet dwells among the living, in his battling against the world, the flesh, and the devil, rather than a failure on his part, knowing too well what would have been the awful result, seeing that the reputation of said Conference, yea, and the whole Connection besides, rested upon his soul in this thing. But this was not all, say, and where would have been that of the consecrated Cross of Christ, his blessed Lord and Master, of whom he had boasted so greatly in gone by days; hence it was here all that the writer regretted was, that he only had but one life to lose in battling in behalf of said Connection and his Lord, believing truly, that if he lost it in this world, that he would find it again in heaven : even so, amen and amen. Hence, we pass by saying, shall Peter bear his cross alone, and all the saints go free ? answer, nay. nay ; as it does truly seem that when there is no cross there can be no crown obtained.

And now, having met said Conference, say, for the fifth annual settlement, in Pittsburg, Pa., say on about the 20th of 10th month, 1849 ; but here it was, to the writer's best recollection on this point, that whereas, the writer's last returns for said year had been principally in that of books and materials, it went, of course, to leave the Conference considerably in arrear, as to his portion for services rendered in his agency, &c. But the understanding was here with the writer, as he did not care to accept either books or materials, to go ahead, and at the next ensuing Conference, to have a final settlement with their faithful and obedient servant, and so give him an honorable acquittal from his field of labour : say, and that probably with an entire family suit of clothing, as a mere compliment. Even so.

Hence, the writer having received his sixth and last annual appointment, he departed for the West, say, to Newark, Ohio, to his ever and esteemed friends, namely, H. R. and family, yea, and that friends indeed, where he had left some few of his things, &c. that he had need of for his winter tour ; but here it was, when he was brought to reflect upon his pecuniary condition, really as it was, without any further disguise before the public or his loving friends, as follows :

First, as before named, in his collecting those books and materials, that required no little labour in packing and leaving them at certain points where they could be readily shipped to this city : yea, so much so, that his physical strength was well nigh done out, from the fact that his limbs would pain him so severe of nights, that he could not rest for weeks.

Secondly, and in keeping his books well posted up in regard to his cash matters for some five years, without any aid whatever.

only of his blessed Lord. Hence, judge ye, dear reader, how it must have been with the writer's brain or nervous system.

Thirdly, and of his own pecuniary circumstances, they being very limited by this; and besides, he had not seen his loving little ones for some several months, whilst the dreary winter was just about set in.

Fourthly, and here having made his calls generally throughout the West on his friends, white and colored, in regard to his agency, it of course, went to cloud his way, and so shut out from him the last ray of hope, as it were, not leaving, say the very first star of all the heavens by which he might only see to steer his poor weather-beaten bark from the impending storm, yea, and from running hard on to some dreadful rock or shoal.

Fifthly, and in addition to all this, he had to foot it, say, from five to six thousand miles per year, or otherwise, he could not have saved the very first cent towards the supporting of his dear little family, of the amount allowed him for his services. But this was not the painful part on this point, it was here he had by this of the many years resorting to his own resources, say, and that of his hard earnings in New Orleans, La., his old and fortunate home, had well nigh failed him, say, as in the case of the poor widow's handful of meal in the barrel, &c. Say, and will his loving readers, right here, before we go further, only for a moment imagine themselves to be in said pitiful condition, yea. and they having no eye to pity, or confidential friend to whom they might look to in said case, &c. But this was not all, for the dreadful dagger is yet to be unsheathed; hence, are you ready to hear it ? and to know, yea, of a truth, that the way to heaven is not on flowery beds of ease. Nay, nay.

Sixthly, and lastly, upon this most heart-rending crisis, and so pass on to the dreadful battle-field, hence comes the fatal stroke. It was this, his wife could not read writing, hence, before he would let the left hand know of that of the right in this case, or before he would have his private letters read, and the contents known by others, he would as soon die. Therefore, the dear reader may plainly see where the dagger found its way to the writer's heart, and there remained broken off, he having none to whom he might in confidence pour out his heart and soul's complaint. Hence, would it not be well for parents to know of a truth that their daughters can both read and write before they dare consent to have them united to any worthy or smart man in marriage, as the writer is perfectly satisfied that in said case, that it is one of the most unequal yokes upon all the face of God's earth; yea, and from said unhappy fate, the very best and the most able men in business upon earth, has been brought down to their untimely graves in sorrow, or otherwise to the Insane Asylum, say, a mere hiss or sport for others, as in the case of poor Samson, with his darling Delilah. Hence, we pass by saying, will all mothers see to this, on the part of their dear daughters, and not to be careful in their being dressed up in their hoop poles, whalebones, oyster shell bonnets, flying ribbons, rose bushes, and earrings almost big enough for rats and mice to jump through, head and tail, without touching, but rather regard them for the purpose which God intended them.

> Hence, to the battle field we go,
> To measure arms with Satan, our greatest foe.
> Nothing to wish, dread or fear,
> If God in presence be ever near.
> Not even to regard our children's cry,
> For if in this we portray our trust we shall for ever die.
> Hence, who with Peter can truly say,
> Lord, I know thou art the way;
> Hence, of thy cup let me drink,
> That I may be snatched from ruin's brink.
> For now it is salvation's come,
> That by the Cross it may be won.
> Hence, on thy hand write my name,
> For one who'll bear thy cross, despise the shame.
> Even so, hallelujah, praise God all ye his loving saints,
> For such a general in the field,
> Who would sooner die than yield.

Now he having taken his leave of said family of Newark, he made for Cleveland, O., and some few other towns thereabouts, and then to Buffalo, N. Y. And here he tarried for some several days with his old time friend, namely, T. T., and made many calls in the way of his agency, but hardly got five dollars. The excuse by some was, that the writer should have staid in Ohio; whilst others thought that each State should provide for her own free negroes, and not to have agents running all over the land under any such pretence. So by this, the writer got tired of said city, and did earnestly pray God to help him in strength to get out of it. But by this there had fallen a deep snow, which made it no little laborious, he being on foot from morning until night, say, and from day to day.

But here, as to his failure in said city, he charged it all to satan, he being well aware of his intent in this his last round. Hence, he having left said city, he thought fit to cross over to her Majesty's province, namely, Upper Canada. But in this it was a failure also, as he merely got his lodging, and about fifty cents. So in this it would truly seem that satan had crossed over before him, as he waits not for ferry boats, in order to accomplish his hellish designs—nay, nay, seeing that he is the Prince of the air, and rides thereon.

But here, without further disguise, say by this the writer was well nigh done out, yea, from the very fact that his heart had began to swell with anguish and pain, not knowing hardly what coast upon earth to steer up his poor tottering bark, or house of clay. And here one thing that made it so hard, he had barely collected enough to meet his real wants on the way, yea, and would sometimes have to go almost barefooted in the snow, about knee deep. But he having crossed back again, he went on down to Niagara Falls; and here, in calling on a certain white family, and having made known to them of his mission, and of his most severe suffering in the cold, and that nearly to the death, the oldest daughter, it seemed, gave him a five dollar piece, and the other members of said family about fifteen dollars, which went to create no little thankfulness of heart, yea, so much so, that he could not refrain from weeping, even in their presence, for such unexpected success in one house, which of course, caused the writer to pour out his very soul in blessings upon said benevolent family, whose names he cannot here recollect; but God in heaven will know them, even in everlasting blessings upon their loving heads ; even so, amen, and selah.

But now, the writer having taken his leave of said family, he sought for some where to put up for the night, where he truly realized more rest than he had nearly for three weeks before, his heart having become assuaged of its anguish and grief ; and so next morning he left for Lockport, N. Y., from thence to Batavia, and so on to Rochester. But on all this route he done mere nothing but wade through the snow from farm to farm on the way; as by this satan having become more and more intent in meting out his hellish purposes, and so defeat the poor weather-beaten herald of the cross of Christ, if possible, and accordingly, did the writer become more fixed in heart and determined to re-sist him by the grace of God to the very hatch gates of hell, or his infernal regions of despair; yea, and there and then to mea-sure arms with him, as in the case of the immortalized Garibaldi, at the battle of St. Angelo, or thereabouts, when upon having met the great chieftain of the Neapolitan army, his opponent de-manded of him to surrender, but in the place of him surrendering, he met him with drawn sword in hand, and he having made a stroke at said Garibaldi with the intention of cutting off his head, Gari-baldi warded off the dreadful blow with his left hand, and with his sabre in the right smote him down, even from his horse to the ground. Hence, it is after this very wise must Lucifer be met, in a spiritual point of view, by every chieftain or hero of the cross of Christ, and by said cross the battle must be won or lost, then it is that ye have fought the good fight of faith. Hence, this dreaming, talking, singing, and shouting about God and Liberty, all avails nothing. For instance, suppose the humble penman had left his liberty to said airy imaginations during the absence of his master, Richard Clague, Esq., of New Orleans, La., say to old England eighteen months, and he had not redeemed said time in working out his liberty, as strictly set forth in the Midnight Cry, say, where might he have been now? answer, probably in some cotton field, sugar farm, or rice pond.

But here, lest we be tedious, or keep the loving reader in further suspense, we hasten on to the great and most miraculous catas-trophe that happened to the writer, as in the case of Job, &c. Hence, he having left Rochester, he next called at Syracuse, and from thence to Peterboro' where he called on his honor G. S. who gave him five dollars. But here he having met with a friend from Salem, Mass., who cordially commended him to go right on to Boston, Mass., and to call on his Excellency, the Governor of the State, namely, G. N. B., and if possible, procure a few lines of him, that would go to give him access to the community throughout said State, and elsewhere down Eastward, &c. until he should be fully enabled to realize the amount required to meet the great and most desired object; even so. He next called at Utica, but here out of all his calls, he did not collect the first cent; and besides, by this, one of the very demons, probably Moloch, cried out distinctly, "Damn it, why don't thee give up the struggle, and go home to thy family, and see to their wants, before they be dragged off to the poor house; and where will be thy heroism then, before the community? will it not be written against thee from every pulpit throughout all Bethel, 'He that provides not for his own house is worse than an infidel.'" And right here, to tell the whole truth, and lie not before his God, as he can profit nothing thereby, he came well nigh of yielding within his heart to satan, on this severe and sore point of temptation. But when upon fasting, and steady prayer for about three days, in accordance with the adorable Trinity, he was truly revived; thus, by the inexpressible grace of God, that he should only remember that he was to be thoroughly sifted in this particular, as in the case of Job. Hence, it was to conquer here the world, the flesh, and the devil, or die, yea, and that for ever, as a traitor to his trust, as in the case of Benedict Arnold. Therefore, will all ye money-called and men-commissioned pulpit leeches, or as it is written in Job xii. 6, "tabernacle of robbers," yea, so much so, that it is in the opinion of the ready writer to be one of the most God provoking causes that now invades this our Christian land, say, from Jackson's Monument, New Orleans, La. to that of Bunkerhill, Boston, Mass., for what care said robbers and pulpit fleecers for the oppressed of our land and the cries of God's poor, whilst they are permitted to go on in purchasing farms, houses and lots, and other real estate, annually to the amount of thousands and thousands of dollars, and besides the millions of dollars worth of unnecessary superfluity, that is actually worn by professors in the house of God, which, if it was only duly appropriated now as in the days of the Apostles, would go to create, no doubt, a common fund, to the amount of some several hundred millions of dollars, that might truly lead to the salvation of this lovely land and nation; seeing that salvation is solely of the Lord, hence it must needs commence in bringing about said deliverance right at the pulpit or the sacred desk, that has been duly dedicated unto the God of all love and liberty.

Say, and will those to whom the writer has here truly appealed see to the matter right now, and so have the trumpet of the great and glorious Jubilee sounded throughout all our land, within twenty-one years at most ; or shall the humble penman here let it be written against them, as in the case of Eli's sons, namely, Hophni and Phinehas. Read the first book of Samuel or Kings, second chapter, and in particular the 29th verse thereof, and so on to the final fate of said priest, and so pass on.

And now, having resolved fully in his heart to die rather than to give up, or to leave the battle field, being cowardly whipped out by satan, there was a sudden ray of light sprung up to his view, thus thinking that if he could only reach Boston, and there only to obtain a few lines from said Governor, that all would be well, as he might then with the greatest propriety, yea, and an assurance rely on his friends, commonly called Quakers, and others that might happen in or on his way from meeting to meeting among said friends, even so ; and for which the writer came to the conclusion as advised by said friend, from Salem, Mass., to take the cars right off for Boston, if it took the very last cent he had collected, &c. But here, in having taken the cars for said city, it did truly seem to him that satan must have taken the very next vacant seat, from the very fact, of all the awful feelings that came upon the writer he never felt so bad before, nay not since the day he made his peace with his God, in Fredericksburg, Va., as strictly set forth in the Midnight Cry, &c. Yea, his feelings became so terrific, that his heart began again to swell with that degree of anguish and pain that he became nearly choked or strangled for the want of being able to breathe. But here, having arrived at Albany, N. Y., say about sun set, he had to change cars, and in calling at the Post Office, he found a letter, by some means or other, had actually been mailed on to said city for him, in which he found as satan had said, that his little ones were about to be taken to the poor house for protection, if not otherwise provided for. Say, dear reader, what now, seeing that your old war-horse and battle axe, as it were, is truly here in a strait, or screwing vice, as it were, and what shall be done now ? Do you say, hang upon the promises of God's grace, or to curse him now, and die. Speak out, all you his loving saints, that are battling for the kingdom of God and everlasting life—as saith the poet.

Am I a soldier of the cross,
  A follower of the Lamb?
And shall I fear to own his cause,
  Or blush to speak his name?
Must I be carried to the skies,
  On flowery beds of ease?
Whilst others fight to win the prize,
  And sail through bloody seas.

But let us return to the point at issue, and say, was God's grace all sufficient at this sore crisis? answer, it was, more than ever, from the fact that it came to the writer's mind thus, that if his little ones did go to the poor-house, to remember that they would be well provided for by his loving friends, namely, the Quakers, who had fed and clothed thousands of the like poor and destitute colored children, and that God would enable them to provide for many more, even so, and for which may God of his ever goodness open the windows of heaven in lasting showers of blessings upon them as a body, or branch of Zion. Selah.

And now, having left Albany for said city of his destination, behold it came to pass, say on or about the 27th of 12th month, A. D. 1849, in having passed the State line station between New York and Massachusetts, say about eight o'clock, P. M. when a most terrific shock smote him right upon the crown of his head, and afterwards, a vivid ray of light of purple color, leaving an awful sense of feeling upon the writer's person, yea, so much so, that within about five minutes after, he found himself to be stiff throughout all his whole body, yea, so much so, that he truly concluded that it certainly was a stroke of death, whilst by this his bones were all burning and aching within, and his hands were here holding on to the seat front of him with a cold deathly grasp, yea, so that he was here constrained to cry out from his inmost soul, O, thou God of heaven! is this death? if so, I am done, and the victory is won, even so, amen, and amen; for to live is Christ, but to die is gain. But right here the writer was made to know sensibly from whence came the mighty shock, in an answer to his interrogation, thus responded the infernal fiend:

"It is me!"

Question, "In the name of God who art thou?"

"Lucifer is my name, yea, the prince of the air, and the ruler of this low world, and hitherto have I come to attest thy love to God and his cause, as in the case of Job : therefore, be it known unto thee, that if thy fidelity in truth be more to thy espoused Prince of Heaven than to all on earth, or any thing it can afford, thou shalt this night be quit thy last claim upon earth, even to thy ten finger nails, and a shaved head, or by all the several foul powers of hell, thou art my prisoner !''

"Even so mote it be," replied the writer, only claiming as an armistice, say until the midnight hour, when he should have received an answer from his Lord and Prince of Glory, in grace, and that he would in the name of Him that said, that "he that will lose his life for my sake shall find it," meet the demand in letter and to the spirit. Amen.

To this demand the proud fiend agreed, hence the writer here became somewhat relieved of said inexpressible excruciating feelings, as before named, until he came to Pittsfield, Mass., say on or about the hour of ten o'clock, P. M., where he concluded to get out and put up for the night, and so prepare to meet his fate, yea, if it was to leave this for another world, only to go bedecked with the scars of honor before the Throne of inspection of his Royal Prince, and there be conducted to a seat, accordingly, in the presence of all the olden time heroes of the cross of Christ that we read of, too tedious here to mention.

So we pass to notice next the dreadful and most miraculous event that occurred between the writer and satan. But here, before we enter the battle field, say, may the humble penman here entreat with his loving readers only to suffer him to speak, and after he has spoken, if ye will mock, then mock on, only that ye mock not to your own hurt or folly. Hence, he having arrived at said town, and the cars having stopped, he here, in leaping from the cars, was smitten to the ground, by an invisible stroke, into the snow, about knee deep, and here, upon rising to his feet, he was smitten down the second time, and when upon rising again, he was here nearly crushed up against the stone wall, so by this the writer was brought to tremble, yea, and to stagger around like unto a drunken man. But here after a while he found his way to the house of a colored family, where he was most kindly received and entertained for the night, but their names he does not here recollect, he having introduced himself to them in particular, when having named to them that he was on his way to Boston, to see said Governor, on some particular business, which of course went to entitle him to their confidence as a stranger. But dear souls, little did they think of the dreadful conflict that was to befall their poor visitor, even that night; nay, nay. Hence, they having blessed their stranger to a good warm supper, he had prayer with them, and having sung a hymn, they kindly conducted him to his retirement, that might be truly called a garden of Gethsemane to him, as follows: Say, it being now about half past eleven o'clock, leaving but a few more moments to decide the poor penman's fate, therefore to prayer; Israel pray whilst your young David shall assault Goliath, the winged fiend of darkness, he having nothing to fight with but Christ the Lord, yea, the little white stone upon which are all the names of saints written since the day that Adam fell. Hence, pray ye children, pray, believing that God, your heavenly Father, has never left himself without living witnesses of his power and saving grace. Even so, amen, and halleluajh, praise his holy name.

And now, he having fell on his knees by the bed side, as truly for the last time in this low world, before his God he prayed thus: "O thou God of all goodness, love and power, grant to this thy servant even grace this night to answer grace, that he may in the name of his Lord, and of his consecrated cross, conquer both earth and hell by a celestial power, and for said victory will he, on his part, meet the demands of satan to the letter and to the spirit thereof, in even giving up his two dear children (himself being understood), namely Julia and Joseph, as a living sacrifice upon thy altar, O God, and for which let it be recorded in heaven and known to the ends of the earth. Even so, amen and amen, and selah." And here, he having met the demands of satan fully in heart, soul, mind and spirit, it was in this did the writer drink of the cup of his Lord and master, in which was truly mingled all of the very dregs of satan's last vial of wrath: yea, so much so, that by the time he had barely rose from the floor, and laid himself upon the bed, when in midst of his inexpressible anguish of soul and mind, as is truly explained in his major Journal, there occurred a sudden crash or explosion in his head, yea, and so dreadful and terrific was the shock that he truly thought that his skull was split wide open, and that his very brain was all out upon the neat snow white pillow cases, which was all the writer here regretted, knowing that he had virtually sealed his life to the support of the cross of Christ. But in raising himself up in the bed to feel for his brains, as he thought, in feeling out on the pillows he felt none, and here upon feeling his skull he found it to be all right; and now, being entirely free from all fear, pain or anguish, of soul, body, yea, and of mind and spirit, he was made to inquire from his inmost soul, and what did this inexpressible sense of inward joy and gladness mean? The reply from heaven was, that in his sacrifice upon the altar of his God, in the support of his holy word, as in the case of Job, it had robbed all hell of its expectation, yea, and had disthroned satan of his cruel power, and hence, the great and glorious victory may be chanted by all God's saints, as follows, as set forth in the Midnight Cry:

Victory o'er the World, the Flesh, and the Devil.

By Faith we conquer earth and hell,
  By a celestial power,
Hence this the grace that shall prevail
  In a decisive or dying hour.

Hence, how dare any man to profane the sacred desk in preaching Christ to be the power of God unto salvation to every one that believeth, when he himself will not trust in Him south of Mason & Dixon's line, as he should, as in the case of Daniel in the lion's den, and Shadrach, Meshach and Abednego, when in the fiery furnace, in the city of Babylon; or otherwise, is not his services thus rendered in the house of God any thing less than a sacrilegious performance, an offering unto devils upon their shrine or hecatombs, being works without faith, which are dead, yea, truly so. Hence should not all such be called in question, for why should our land be cursed any further, as in the case of Jezebel and her 400 lying prophets.

It was just about the midnight hour,
When Jesus displayed his heavenly power,
And with his chariot drove along,
While Angels chanted the morning song.

His lightning played and thunders roll,
It shook the earth from pole to pole.
At this the devils took affright,
And left before the morning light.

As Zion's sons marched in and took the field,
Old Moloch of hell was the last devil to yield;
And with a most tremendous yell,
He leap'd from thence down to hell.

And here with Job I was called to stand,
And show myself a worthy man;
Thus born of God, I know I am,
And thou, deny it if thee can.

Hence, in compliance with God's command,
I'm certainly bound for Canaan's land;
Even so—Salvation, O the bleeding Lamb. Selah.

And next comes the recompense of the great reward, if faithful until death, as follows:—Installed as a prince of Jerusalem, and a warrior that of a knight of the consecrated cross of Christ, the Prince of Glory, and that of eternal life. Amen, and amen.

Hence, judge ye by this ye little flock of heaven, if ye have not one who has in deed and in truth measured arms with all hell, and claims himself to be a Washington and a Garibaldi for his King, the only heir of all heaven, yea, life and liberty; though he be left to wander up and down with a shaved head, owing to said mighty shock, that satan left him as a sore scar in attest of the battle fought; yea, in being so severe that it actually shattered the nervous system of the brain, as thought by his physician, probly for ever in this world, as the writer is now rather advanced in years, say, in his 47th, as may be seen strictly set forth in the Midnight Cry, yea, truly so, so we pass from this to a complete triumph in a temporal point of view, and we have done with the proposed Narrative.

And now the writer having been duly crowned, as it were, with a wreath of twelve stars, in token of the battle thus fought and the victory won, as before named, he carrying the scars of honor accordingly on his person until this day, say the 25th of 12th month, A. D. 1860, since the Christian era had its origin, even so, namely, a shattered nervous system of the brain, going continually with a shaved head, with a white spot of hair, in attest of the severe neuralgia in the head, occasioned by said dreadful shock upon the brain, he being now left to wander up and down through all the land clad more or less with dead friends clothing, as in the case of that of Elisha being truly clad with his father Elijah's mantle, and with it did he truly whip out or cause to to separate the water of the river Jordan, and conquered all earth and hell besides, and so found his way up to the portals of the skies, upon which Job's character may be seen written out, it does truly seem in four large brilliant stars, entitled Job's Coffin; he claiming not where of his own upon which he may rest the sole of his foot, only as named in the Midnight Cry. Notwithstanding all this, yet is his hope in the holy word of God, namely, the 71st and 91st Psalms of King David, stronger than ever ; yea, so much so, that he has truly come to the conclusion to patiently wait upon the Lord, even his God, all of his appointed days, until his change come, he believing without a shadow of doubt that all things in the end thereof shall have worked together for his good, even so may God in his promised mercy grant. Amen, and amen.

And now, he having truly drank to the very dregs of the hot cup of satan's vindictive wrath, and the most dreadful feelings having all as a mighty thunder storm passed over, he rested for the remainder of the night as though he was reposing upon one of the richest sofas all earth could afford him, whilst that of his heavenly visions and conversation in heaven or the spirit world, probably it would not be here right or lawful to name. So we pass in saying that, having arose in the morning, his loving host desired of course to know how he rested during the night; he gladly answered as to the latter part, but to the fore part he thought it prudent not to let the left hand know of that of the right in this case; for instance, had not Samson revealed to his darling

Delilah wherein his great strength lay, he might have escaped his untimely death.

Hence, he having spent about the happiest first day here on earth with said kind family, on second day morning he gave the Episcopal priest a call in behalf of his mission, who did most cordially, yea, and liberally aid him in advising as follows: that all the free colored people of these United States should be shipped off to Africa, but did not name what should be done with the three or four millions of slaves of the South. As it seemed that some of the clergy of the North, had not got tired out in supping of the molasses of Louisiana, and of eating of the product of the sweatened rice ponds of South Carolina, and other rich staples from that source. Hence, if the writer may be permitted to judge in this partiular, was it not the design to clear the United States of all the free colored people, so that thousands of others might be imported from the shores of Africa to the Southern market, and so establish their belief that slavery on the part of that race is a peculiar Divine Institution, and so nail said traffic, with all of its inexpressible horrors, on to the cross of Christ, who truly said, that thou shalt love the Lord thy God with all thy heart, and thy neighbour as thyself, and afterward sealed it to his cross with his dying breath, and so bade his loving flock adieu, until he shall come again in his everlasting kingdom of grace, and those who have faitfully adhered to said commandments, and none other, shall be permitted to drink with him the cup of love anew. Even so, in his holy name may it be, in token of his dying love written upon the table of every true believers heart, and sealed with his blood upon the cross. Even so, praise God, all ye his faithful children. Amen, and selah.

And now, having left said village for Boston, and having made some several calls in the towns or villages on the way, his success was beyond all expectation, from the fact, that by the time he had arrived at good old Cambridge, Mass., and there having called on his Honor, E. E., who did most readily and liberally sign in behalf of the support of the poor agent's Mission, which caused others to subscribe who saw his name and donation, say about $200. Judge ye by this, ye loving readers, how the writer must have felt in body and mind in consequence of so miraculous a change in favor of one poor mortal, say in this the age of our world 5864 years, since the day in which the morning stars sang together, and the sons of God shouted for joy, as has been strictly written out in the Midnight Cry, &c. Hence, may the blessings of God await him throughout the remainder of his journey towards his long home, namely, by the grace of God a peaceful grave. And here, before we pass, in justice to his honor, of no liittle merit and due qualification, in the opinion of the writer, had he only been elected President, and a Vice President from Louisiana, as captain and mate upon the old ship, that must soon start, as it were, for a four years voyage. Say, and in this, would not old Bunker Hill, Mass., and Jackson's Monument, La. have shook hands together; hence, what could the body have done under heaven but adhere, in obedience to the head and foot, in this all momentous case before us; and that probably with no little lamentation ere long, as none but God, in the humble opinion of the writer, can possibly avert the impending storm, that does so blacken the heavens, and cover the earth with thick darkness; yea, so much so, that it is no little felt by every true and devoted lover of his country. And for which will the writer here pray the Lord, even his God, yea, and that of Elijah, that whereas, he has truly stirred up the great bald Eagle's nest, as it were, even from New Orleans to Boston, yea, and that to a true sense of their danger, without thy helping hand to deliver them; therefore, O thou God of all love and long forbearance, yea, and most generously waiting still to be gracious and merciful unto this thy people, as thou hast been in the days of thy servant George, as in the case where thou didst deliver thy people of old, even Israel, by the hand of thy servant Moses, and wilt thou here, of thine inexpressible, ever abounding love and compassion, spare this, thy favored fig tree yet another and another year, so that thy faithful servants throughout this our land may dig about its roots, and so lop off all the dead and unnecessary limbs, that doth so hurtfully encumber it, that it cannot bear that sweet and most delicious fruit of love and liberty to all men alike, without distinction as to nation, climate or color; and if it then bear said fruit to meet the end for which it was truly intended by thy divine Providence, that thou shouldest reserve it as an eagle's nest unto thy Christ, even our Lord and great salvation, well; but if not, then thy holy word for it. Even so, amen, selah.

And now, having called on his excellency, the Governor G. N. B., at the Adams House, Washington Street, Boston, on or about the 14th or 15th of 1st month, A. D. 1850, and he there and then having spread out all his credentials before his honour, and he having seen the signature of his old school mate, namely, his excellency, Governor Z. F. of Ohio, as before named, he was no little amused and well pleased, yea, so much so, that he did most readily endorse the same, which of course went to open the way throughout all the old Bay State, in favor of his agency, yea, so much so, though strange to say, yet in truth, the further he went down East the more liberal he found the Friends to be, and others whom he might happen to call on, they being on his way in keeping in strict range with the meetings with said Friends, as far down as Lubec, Maine, as follows: say, commencing at Lynn, Mass., where, and in the neighbourhood, he collected about $160; yea, and there and then did he deposit it in bank as fast as he collected it, getting drafts for the same to the order of Hanson Johnson, Treasurer of the said Institute, which his books here will show in attest of the fact thereof. And here, to his still greater surprise, when having reached Salem, the city from which said friend hailed who did so kindly recommend that the writer, when amidst his deepest distress, should call on said Governor, and sure enough, it was just as he said. Hence, who here, of all his loving readers, would doubt for a moment, that said friend or messenger was not so ordered by an all-wise Providence to meet his servant on the way in order to strengthen him, yea, and to confirm his hope in his holy Word, as in the most noted case of Abraham, when he was met by a friend and stranger right from Salem, to bless and to comfort him, when after a most desperate struggle in the behalf of Lot, his nephew, &c. For lo, here it was to his inexpressible joy and gladness of heart, did he actually collect in one day about 90 or 100 dollars, and for which may it ever be a city of peace and brotherly love, as the Salem of old. Even so, amen, and selah.

But here before we pass, the writer would merely ask the dear reader, what think ye in truth of so great and miraculous a change in his favor thus? yea, so much so, that for joy he became almost insensible to the cold and the snow through which he had to wade from day to day, being about two feet deep, or up to the knees. For instance, when upon having got down in the State of Maine say to Waterville meeting of Friends, on the Kennebec river, and here he having become acquainted with some of the members of said meeting, namely, J. D. L. and S. T., who did on first day preach one of the most delightful discourses that he has ever heard, since the discourse delivered by a Baptist minister, Dr. McCall, under which he got converted from his sins, in Fredericksburg, Virginia, say on or about the 10th of 8th month, A. D. 1831, as has been duly set forth in the Midnight Cry, &c. And here, he was most cordially received by them, and they and others of said meeting became properly acquainted with the writer and the object of his mission. But here, what went to make his mission with them of no little importance, and highly worthy of their liberal patronage was this, they having seen what the several meetings of Friends of Ohio had done in cash, and that of Pennsylvania, and good old New Jersey, say, beginning at Mount Pleasant, Ohio, with his kind old friend and household, namely, D. U., yea, and there were many others thereabouts who were determined not to be left behind in this heaven-favored race that was so plainly set before them in running for the kingdom, seeing that in this race all might run, and obtain a prize in proportion to their merits. Even so. Hence, judge ye by this, how the loving Friends of said meeting and others thereabouts must have felt in this matter, as the writer collected about $500. In consequence of which, he became so overwhelmed with joy and peace in the Holy Ghost, that he nearly became insensible to the cold, as before named. But here, what do the loving readers say, as regards God's grace and power on those whom he loves? say, and is he indeed a present help in the time of need on the part of his little ones? Hence, we pass by saying, may God ever remember said meeting, and others, in lasting blessings upon their loving and devoted heads. Even so, amen, and selah.

Hence, he being here advised to give the Friends a visit about ten miles or so West of Augusta, the Capital of said State, before he went further down, he started for said meeting accordingly, early in the morning across the Kennebec, on the ice, on a 20 or 30 miles march, through snow knee deep, almost barefooted, as his boots, being much worn, scarcely afforded any protection. Having reached his destination about sunset, he called on A. S., who carries on about one of the largest oil cloth factories probably in the State of Maine, and who received him kindly, and invited him to stay all night. So, after a good hearty supper, as the writer had eaten nothing that day, having merely drank a little good old rye, as a protection against the severe cold. His host, having noticed the condition of the writer's boots, said to him : "Friend Wilkerson, I would like to ask thee a question."

Reply.—"Say on."

Host.—" In looking over thy book, it seems that thou must have collected some eight or nine hundred dollars ?"

Reply.—"Yea, say about one thousand dollars, as the last check will show."

Host.—"Do thy employers allow thee nothing for thy services?"

Reply.—" They do ; but that is a future thought."

Host.—" But here, what I wish to get at is this, how is it, that thou having all of said amount of money in thy possession, and here I have been observing thy feet to be nearly bare ; say, how is it ?"

Reply.—" It is thus : I am not soliciting aid of my Quaker friends to purchase $30 cloaks, $20 coats, $5 hats, $7 boots, shirts $12 per dozen, and to cap the climax, a horse and buggy for $100 ; but rather to erect some several good neat log buildings on the farm, that is truly intended as a shelter or an Orphan's Asylum. To meet said object have I been laboring thus, for these six long years, asking nothing more on earth than only to live to see its completion, if afterwards I have to be buried with a dead man's shirt on. Even so, amen, and amen."

Host.—" That is enough, I now see the drift plainly, therefore, in the morning thou shalt have my boots to put on, until thine is well mended."

Hence, in the morning the writer was directed where to go to get his boots mended, and besides a number of names given him, so that he might be collecting among the Friends whilst his boots were being repaired ; in that day he collected about $20. Having returned to said friend and reported his great success, he put his hand in his pocket, and gave him a ten dollar bill. God bless him and all his house, the fifty or sixty factory hands being understood.

Now, having taken his leave of said meeting, he went as far down as Lubec, Maine, and in this place his success with the

Friends in their meeting was about as heretofore, but by this time their meetings had become small; nevertheless, they were both liberal and kind. Hence, will not God of his abundant grace bless them for this act of duty towards his poor? he will. Therefore, loving Friends, who did so kindly and liberally sustain the humble writer, as before named, you have his prayers and best wishes, and he cannot find words to express his deep and abiding sense of gratitude.

Perhaps some of his loving readers may here ask, why was not the writer in all this long romantic tour heard from, either in lecturing or preaching, or through some newspaper that might be favorable to his mission? Answer, because during said period of his most bitter affliction, he was ever found occupying an humble position with the Friends in their meetings, in silence before his God, in deep meditation of his inexpressible goodness in having thus blessed his efforts; besides, the mental powers of the writer were somewhat impaired, and it was necessary that he should keep as quiet as possible throughout this trying period of his journey through life.

And now, he having arrived at Lubec, even down on the sea coast, where he thought fit to embark for Eastport, and from thence he shipped to St. Johns, New Brunswick; and even here, to his no little surprise, did he actually find friends who each gave one pound, which of course, went to make the writer know, even here, that if God was for him, who could be otherwise; say, hear it, ye God-fearing children, hear it.

And after remaining at this place several days, and meeting with considerable success in his mission, he concluded to return to the United States by the interior or land route, but not without commending her Majesty's loving subjects unto God, and his everlasting protection. Even so, amen.

Hence, he having left said city, he came next to Calais, Maine, and here he met with the same friendship and success as heretofore. By this time, the Spring had fully set in, it being about the 30th of 4th month, 1850, when the writer suffered severely in consequence of frosted limbs, which brought him to a true sense of his danger, as the burning and misery was so severe just below the knees, that he really thought that he should lose both legs. But praise be to God, he soon recovered. He here made up his mind to change his mode of travel, by sailing around from island to island, and in this manner he rested from such severe labour. Yet his mental powers were still feeble: he being advancing in years, he had little hope of an increase of strength thereof.

But here, in justice to his friends of Nantucket, though located on a small island, yet they certainly done their part, particularly the kind family with whom he put up, namely, A. W., who seeing that he was nearly destitute of comfortable clothing, did amply supply his wants, particularly with some of the best shirts that he ever had, and for which they, of course, have his thanks and prayers to God in their behalf until this day. Even so, amen.

Having left said island, he sailed next for Long Island, N. Y. Having arrived at Jamaica, he next proceeded to Jericho, where he concluded to remain and reckon up all his books, and so prepare to make his sixth and final Report of his stewardship, that he might be prepared to rest on the seventh year from all his labors. He found the amount collected to be $1375, and in order to make it even $1400, he gave the meeting of Friends at this place a call, and in a day or two, by divine aid, the object was accomplished, and a few cents over. Praise God, ye saints, for in this, has not the battle of the Lord been truly fought, and the victory won, and the long desired object attained at last. Hence, what remains but to praise the Lord, as in the noted cases of his servants of old, even King David, the son and stem of Jesse, when upon taking up the ark of the covenant from Shiloh up to Jerusalem, the chosen city of the most high God, yea, the God of Abel, Enoch, Noah, Abraham, Isaac, Jacob, Joseph, Moses, Aaron, Joshua, Caleb, Samson, Sarah, Rebecca, Hannah, Samuel, Elijah, Elisha, Daniel, Shadrach, Meshach, Abednego, Isaiah, Jeremiah, Ezekiel, Paul, Peter, James and John, yea, and of the thousands and tens of thousands of his saints, who by faith in God, through Christ Jesus our Lord, conquered all earth and hell, and are now seated at God's right hand.

In attest of the same the writer here sets his seal this 3d day of 1st month, A. D. 1861, and of the World, 5865.

MAJOR JAMES WILKERSON,

Of New Orleans, La., Author of the Midnight Cry.

A Virginian by birth, born not far from Little York, a town of no little renown, and as to his blood, he is of the Bengal of Africa, Anglo-

Saxon of Europe, Powhatton of America; but strictly the grandson of Col. Wilkerson, who fought with one of the bravest of the brave, namely General Gates, at the battle of Saratoga, N. Y.

And now, after some several weeks of delightful rest of body and mind, it being well on to the 1st of 9th month, and time that he should make his return to the Conference, that met about the 20th of the same, he took his leave of said meeting of Friends, yea, and so bade adieu to this ever memorable place of repose, but not until he had first emptied his soul, as it were, of the very last blessing upon said meeting of Friends, and others thereabouts, who did so kindly entertain the writer, a stranger and pilgrim among them.

Hence, he having left said island, he sailed for New York City, where he had all of his checks duly attested by his worthy friend, I. T. H., he having examined them all carefully, according to the very latest Bank Detector, and so made his returns of the amount collected in cash, $1060, besides a land warrant claiming 160 acres, the land warrant being the writer's, and upon which land he truly intended to have established an Auxiliary to the Union Seminary, at some future period, thinking that he might be the means of providing a shelter for the fatherless, and so meet the saying of St. James, as before named. But in this he was disappointed, as will be seen in the conclusion. So we proceed by saying, that all said amount and land warrant were duly received by said Treasurer, as his books will show. Even so; so far so good.

This being settled, he now concluded, in order to improve his health, that he would embark for Matanzas or Havana, Cuba, and from thence on to Kingston, Jamaica, and then to Chagres, Central America, where he had purposed to spend the ensuing Winter with an old friend of his, namely, Joseph Prince, and for him to have acted as recording clerk, for $100 per month and found, he having received information to that effect by a particular friend. But in this quite cheering expectation he was sadly disappointed, from the very fact, that he having purchased the land warrant out of his quota due him for services, and besides, he sent on $128 of the remainder to make up the sum of $1060, as before stated; and further, having purchased for himself a suitable coat to travel in; so when he arrived at Havana, and met all the necessary expenses there, he found that he actually had not enough funds left him to get as far as Kingston, Jamaica. Hence, he concluded to have his passport endorsed for New Orleans, La., where he landed, after a most delightful sail, about the 1st of 11th month, 1850. But he had not money enough to pay his passage on the packet Adam Gray, being $30, for which purpose he pawned his lever watch for five or six dollars. Now in order to get back his watch, and means sufficient to go to Louisville, Ky., without asking aid of the brethren or the church, he disguised himself, and went about the city sawing wood, as a mere stranger, not letting the left hand know the secrets of the right, lest his pecuniary condition might become known throughout the city, and his loving sisters, who knew him of old, and of his labours of love in behalf of the sacred and loving cause of dear Zion, should become, as it were, almost frantic in their efforts to raise the means to help him out of his difficulties. They would also naturally be anxious to know the cause of his long absence, say about eleven years, as may be seen by his dear readers, by carefully observing the commencement of this Narrative. Even so. Hence, we proceed, by saying that in said disguised condition, did he soon earn enough to get his watch, yea, and besides, to pay his way up to Louisville, Kentucky, on the steamer General Lafayette. But here, the writer, before leaving New Orleans, would express his gratitude to G. Smith and his dear family, where he stopped, who generously gave him a five dollar hat, and some shirts. God bless them.

Hence, he now having taken his leave of his almost idolized home, and having embarked upon said steamer for Louisville, he was treated with no little kindness by both the captain and steward all the way up to said city. Even so; may God bless them.

Having arrived at Louisville, he was received by the church and brethren, and that without distinction as to sect or color, yea, so much so, that he here having merely named his limited circumstances, when the worthy brother in charge, namely, II. R. R., took up a collection of about thirty dollars, in order to get him a good suit of Winter clothing made; and whilst this was being done, the other kind brother over in Jeffersonville, Indiana, namely, J. A. W., even put his very best over-coat upon his poor old brother and fellow soldier, in order to defend him from the cold and dreary Winter, until such time as his own should be ready. Hence, he would pray that the Lord his God would bless his servants for such acts of kindness bestowed upon the chosen and faithful standard bearer of His most precious and holy word, throughout all this beloved land, as has been most faithfully set forth in the Midnight Cry, as a truthful warning. And further, he would pray with all his heart that peace may be multiplied unto said city, and unto all the towns thereabout, that did participate in this thing; and that, as the hen gathereth her tender brood under her wings to save them from the storm, ye may all be gathered together under the protecting wings of the Almighty; and that the inhabitants of dear old St. Louis, Mo., may be included in said blessing. Even so, amen, and selah.

He next visited Cincinnati, Ohio, where the dear children in Bethel truly seemed as if they did not wish to be left behind in so good a cause. Even so, come in, and share alike with all the rest of the dear little brood, as you will not be excluded on account of color. Nay, nay.

The writer next visited Wheeling, Virginia, where he made his head quarters, it being one of the choicest of all the fig trees in his heavenly Father's garden. Here he tarried until properly rested, about a year or so, as he did truly need it. What say ye, loving readers? think ye not, that if ever human being needed rest, your humble servant did.

At this time he made a visit to Washington, Pa., and to Brownsville, in the same State, where he had a close interview with his beloved friend, namely, Dr. A. S. a cousin to the Quaker lady, namely, Lucy Harris, who educated the humble writer, when but a youth, in Richmond, Va.

But here, it may be asked, "how was said female friend thus permitted to instruct the writer, knowing that the laws of Virginia forbid the like?" answer, it so happened at the time, in the year 1826, that said friend was in prison for an unjust debt that she would not consent to pay, whilst on the part of the humble scribe he was confined there also for having run away. Hence, as there was no law on the part of said State forbidding that he should be taught thus, there could be no transgression, of course; seeing, in the humble opinion of the writer, that said prison in this case, was truly the end of the law for a most righteous and praiseworthy act, on the part of said friend, even L. H.; so the children were free. Even so, amen. For is it not reasonable to suppose that

this ever to be remembered and highly esteemed friend should
Providentially be sent to prison for this very purpose, as in the
case of Esther when called to the Persian Throne, and there installed as Queen; and who afterwards became instrumental in the
redemption of her people Israel. Yea, and that said friend might
there and then light up a candle that should shine before this land
and nation, as of that of the great and worthy hero John Rodgers,
in old England, that has never been snuffed out until this day.
Even so, amen; yea, and let all God's saints say amen, and selah.

Said kind friend was educated in Weston School, Pa., about the
time the two worthy friends, namely, J. E. and his wife, were
teachers therein, say from about the years 1820 to 1830. But
we pass, by saying in all love and due respect to said female and
school, from which source he derived his four months learning,
may the God of all the good and righteous grant that a special
angel may ever abide within her walls, as one of the household,
to shield and defend them from all harm; yea, and that said
School may ever be as a fountain of light and knowledge, from
which may many of God's poor derive a portion therefrom, as in
the case of the writer. Hence, we take our leave of one of the
most Providential circumstances probably on record in this our
Christian land.

As to further particulars on this point, they are all written out
in his Major Journal. Therefore, let us sing unto the Lord as
follows:

God moves in a mysterious way,
His wonders to perform;
He plants his footsteps in the sea,
And rides upon the storm.

Deep in unfathomable mines
Of never-failing skill,
He treasures up his bright designs,
And works his sovereign will.

Ye fearful saints, fresh courage take
The clouds ye so much dread
Are big with mercy—and shall break
In blessings on your head.

Judge not the Lord by feeble sense,
But trust him for his grace;

Behind a frowning providence
He hides a smiling face.

His purposes will ripen fast,
Unfolding every hour ;
The bud may have a bitter taste,
But sweet will be the flower.

Blind unbelief is sure to err,
And scan his work in vain ; ·
God is his own interpreter,
And he will make it plain.

The writer would here observe that some of the great self-styled consequentials of the day looked on the Midnight Cry as mere speculation on God's holy word on the part of the truthful scribe, who never dares to use his pen and ink except for the promotion of the good cause of his blessed Lord 'and master. But here, lest the inquiry should be made from New Orleans, La., to Boston, Mass., "by whom was it so considered?" answer, by him to whom he returned his piece of silver, and that not a thousand miles from Flushing, Ohio.

The writer being informed by said Physician, that in consequence of the disordered state of his brain, it was absolutely necessary that he should retire to some remote place on the sea coast, where he might be benefitted by the salt water. Even so, amen. Otherwise, where would the writer have been this day ?

But here the writer would state to his beloved readers, that worthy physician is no more here to advise or prescribe for his fellow creatures. Nay, nay, for he himself has passed away like a long Summer's day, seeing that with mortal here he could no longer stay. Hence, God grant that it may be all well with his soul. Even so, amen.

So farewell, loving friend, and all thy house, since thy servant, in obedience to thy godly advice, must hasten on.

And now, the writer having faithfully promised to his physician that he would strictly adhere to his directions in this particular, seeing that his only chance of recovery lay therein, he returned to Wheeling, where his friends, white and colored, aided him most liberally. Hence, he made ready to go on to meet the Conference that assembled at Cincinnati, on or about the 25th of 8th month,

A. D. 1852. Having taken leave of his kind friend, namely, E. E. and family, he set out from thence on foot, passing on through several towns, namely St. Clairsville, Washington, Cambridge, Zanesville, and here he tarried over first day, and gave the dear children a missionary discourse, and they, on their part, gave him a liberal collection of about eighteen dollars, to help him on his journey. Even so, may God bless them, and ever save them from false teachers. He also prays that the favor of the Lord may rest with his old friend, W. F., and all his dear family. Here the writer would observe, that if any church in all Bethel has been most grievously fleeced, said church has, as in the case of that at New Orleans; yea, so much so, that it has pleased the Lord, even the writer's God, to save the latter from said infamy in His Holy Temple, and for which has the humble scribe bowed his knees three times, ¡yea, and kissed the very earth seven, in thankfulness of heart. Even so, amen.

He next visited Newark, the town from whence he left for the battle field; and here he had a most precious time with his friend, H. R., and kind family, in relating all that happened to him during his long absence.

From thence, the writer came to this city, and here he having found his friend, H. Johnson and all his family well, and all things pertaining to his trust, worthy, as a faithful Treasurer of the Union Seminary, standing upright to the present time, which of course went to create no little pleasing sensation upon the much afflicted mind of the humble scribe; yea, and for which he was enabled to leave this city for Cincinnati, Ohio, with no little satisfaction, where he met with said Conference. But here he soon found, from the feebleness of his head and mind, that it was really necessary for him to leave all his claims on said Conference for service, and his domestic affairs in their hands, as a body of brethren for whom he had labored thus, and that virtually to the death, as has been stated, claiming nothing further, on the part of said Conference, only reserving the right to attend to his land warrant, and the purpose for which he intended it at a future period, when his mind would permit him to attend to it.

Hence, for all further information, as touching said Orphans' Institute, and of its progress, has not the writer published it from year to year, in some several thousand copies, namely, the Epistles, Addresses, and lastly, the Appeals to said Conference. Hence, the writer having here had a final settlement with said Conference, before named, as the minutes will show, he now of course felt himself much relieved in mind, and was now at liberty to act in accordance with the advice of his worthy physician.

But in the next place, how is the writer to be supported whilst in this feeble state of body and mind? answer, rather than depend upon said Conference for support, he had struck off and sold of

His own Lithograph,	3500, at 40	cents each,	. . .	$1400
Lithograph of B. L.	2500, at 25	do.	. . .	625
G. Epistles,	4000, at 12	do.	. . .	480
Pamphlets,	4000, at 12	do,	. . .	480
Alphabets,	2000, at 15	do.	. . .	300
Epistles and Addresses	3000, at 10	do.	. . .	300

Total Amount $3585

Hence, be it known here on earth, as well as it is known in heaven, that it was after this wise that the writer has duly ministered unto his own wants, as in the case of the apostle Paul, in the last several years of his travelling to and fro through the United States, say from 5000 to 10,000 miles per year, going about, as in the case of his Lord, doing good. Yea, he having of the above sum faithfully divided about $3,300 in cash among the poor widows and orphans, without distinction as to color. Hence, in this particular, was he not a husband to the widow, and a father to the fatherless?

But alas, alas! he has nothing now of all his loaves and fishes left him, but a few copies of his Midnight Cry, that he disposes of in going around. Well, even so, since he feels assured that he will not die for want of bread, whilst his Quaker friends have a shelter for the poor and needy, into which he may enter, and there chop straw and stuff mats through the day, and to lift up his soul by night in thanksgiving unto the Lord his God, for such a shelter in his old days; yea, it being similar to that of his blessed Lord and Master, when born in Bethlehem Judah, the city of David. Even so, amen.

Seeing that said friends have some several shelters thus provided in the City of Philadelphia, yea, and one in particular, near

Willow and Thirteenth Streets, containing annually some seventy or eighty colored orphans, who are well provided for, yea, and besides, they are all well educated. Say, beloved reader, is not this an act of charity on the part of Friends in the behalf of God's poor little brood?

But here, as it might be asked by some one of the writer's friendly subscribers to his Narrative, for what purpose shall the profits thereof go to? answer, if there should be any after all of the necessary expenses are duly settled up, he may probably have need of it himself, to subsist on in his cave, lest he might become a pauper upon the community; and that he would not like to be, seeing that they have about their hands full already, it being solely from neglect on the part of the clergy, as before named. Therefore, should not every religions society within these United States who may be found neglecting their poor widows and orphans, be regarded nothing less than a nest of Infidels? having denied the faith and principles that were taught by the Prophets and Apostles. Yea, a nuisance and a disgrace to the Commonwealth of Israel, and ought to be broken up, accordingly. And, in the opinion of the writer, if there could be some clause to that effect in the Constitution of the United States, it would be no doubt the salvation of this our dear land and nation. Even so, in God's holy name mote it be.

And now, the penman and ready writer having here truly uncased his bosom, and poured out his soul in truth, he can now retire to his cave in peace, yea, and of no little joy in the Holy Ghost. Hence, may he not climb where Moses stood, and see the blessed land, yea, there and then to read his name written upon his Saviour's hand; and with his holy presence bid, let him die as Moses did. Selah.

Do justly, love mercy, and to walk humbly before thy God, oh man! Even so, selah.

And now, in conclusion, if the humble penman has any friends in said Conference, rather than those of Job's comforters, namely, Eliphaz the Temanite, Bildad the Shuhite, and Zophar the Naamathite, say, may he here most respectfully ask of them in God's holy name to do the right and clean thing.

See that Green and Thompson lift their note of $600, with interest thereon, so that there may be some two or three more good log buildings erected on said farm; and also, see that the difference between him and said Conference of $494 03 be paid over to his two children and their mother; and further see that those Trustees in Vanwert, Ohio, give up every acre that was claimed by said land warrant also, to said children and their mother, free of all cost, excepting the tax due thereon to C. D. Young; and in particular, see that all those ministers of said Conference who have gone to Canada, her Majesty's province, to reside, not to concern themselves any further about the property of said Seminary, but rather go to work there, and establish something of the same, and so prove themselves truly worthy of her Royal Majesty's protection; or otherwise, should they be discarded, where upon God's earth will they go?

MILLENIUM, OR 1000 YEARS REST.—Revelations, 20th Chapter.

Oh! thou Holy Dove, sweet messenger of rest,
That descends from above poor mortals to bless;
Come strengthen thy saints in love and in power,
That they may stand and not faint in a most trying hour. Selah.

But lastly, and now to all the saints of the most High God, you are hereby notified, yea, and requested to separate yourselves from any further connection with what is called Free Masonry, in the sacred desk, claiming no other discipline for yourselves in future than the 13th chapter of Romans, for why should you be cursed any further by said infamy in the house of God, that is so well calculated to starve out its thousand of widows and orphans, leaving the oppressed of our land entirely out of the question. Yea, and furthermore, has not said infamy even covenanted with death in God's holy sanctuary, and gone into a written agreement with hell? and for which has not God been provoked to visit this our beloved land and nation, in judgment, the end thereof who knows? For information on this point, let all who will read the 32d chapter of Deuteronomy, and then answer the humble writer, should not the church of God be found in spotless white, as the Lord of all may soon appear. Hence to his sacred cross let all his loving saints now draw near. Amen. And finally farewell, children.

From thy father and servant, for Christ's sake. Selah.

M. J. W. of N. O. La.

www.ingramcontent.com/pod-product-compliance
Lightning Source LLC
Chambersburg PA
CBHW021445090426
42739CB00009B/1656